31

Lectures on the Logic of Computer Programming

ZOHAR MANNA

Stanford University and Weizmann Institute of Science

CBMS-NSF

REGIONAL CONFERENCE SERIES
IN APPLIED MATHEMATICS

SPONSORED BY
CONFERENCE BOARD OF
THE MATHEMATICAL SCIENCES

SUPPORTED BY
NATIONAL SCIENCE
FOUNDATION

CBMS-NSF
REGIONAL CONFERENCE SERIES IN
APPLIED MATHEMATICS

A series of lectures on topics of current research interest in applied mathematics under the direction of the Conference Board of the Mathematical Sciences, supported by the National Science Foundation and published by SIAM.

GARRETT BIRKHOFF, *The Numerical Solution of Elliptic Equations*

D. V. LINDLEY, *Bayesian Statistics, A Review*

R. S. VARGA, *Functional Analysis and Approximation Theory in Numerical Analysis*

R. R. BAHADUR, *Some Limit Theorems in Statistics*

PATRICK BILLINGSLEY, *Weak Convergence of Measures: Applications in Probability*

J. L. LIONS, *Some Aspects of the Optimal Control of Distributed Parameter Systems*

ROGER PENROSE, *Techniques of Differential Topology in Relativity*

HERMAN CHERNOFF, *Sequential Analysis and Optimal Design*

J. DURBIN, *Distribution Theory for Tests Based on the Sample Distribution Function*

SOL I. RUBINOW, *Mathematical Problems in the Biological Sciences*

PETER D. LAX, *Hyperbolic Systems of Conservation Laws and the Mathematical Theory of Shock Waves*

I. J. SCHOENBERG, *Cardinal Spline Interpolation*

IVAN SINGER, *The Theory of Best Approximation and Functional Analysis*

WERNER C. RHEINBOLDT, *Methods of Solving Systems of Nonlinear Equations*

HANS F. WEINBERGER, *Variational Methods for Eigenvalue Approximation*

R. TYRRELL ROCKAFELLAR, *Conjugate Duality and Optimization*

SIR JAMES LIGHTHILL, *Mathematical Biofluiddynamics*

GERARD SALTON, *Theory of Indexing*

CATHLEEN S. MORAWETZ, *Notes on Time Decay and Scattering for Some Hyperbolic Problems*

FRANK HOPPENSTEADT, *Mathematical Theories of Populations: Demographics, Genetics and Epidemics*

RICHARD ASKEY, *Orthogonal Polynomials and Special Functions*

L. E. PAYNE, *Improperly Posed Problems in Partial Differential Equations*

SAUL ROSEN, *Lectures on the Measurement and Evaluation of the Performance of Computing Systems*

HERBERT B. KELLER, *Numerical Solution of Two Point Boundary Value Problems*

J. P. LASALLE, *The Stability of Dynamical Systems*—Z. ARTSTEIN, *Appendix A— Limiting Equations and Stability of Nonautonomous Ordinary Differential Equations*

DAVID GOTTLIEB and STEVEN A. ORSZAG, *Numerical Analysis of Spectral Methods: Theory and Applications*

PETER J. HUBER, *Robust Statistical Procedures*

HERBERT SOLOMON, *Geometric Probability*

FRED S. ROBERTS, *Graph Theory and Its Applications to Problems of Society*

JURIS HARTMANIS, *Feasible Computations and Provable Complexity Properties*

ZOHAR MANNA, *Lectures on the Logic of Computer Programming*

ELLIS L. JOHNSON, *Integer Programming*

SHMUEL WINOGRAD, *Arithmetic Complexity of Computations*

Lectures
on the Logic
of Computer Programming

ZOHAR MANNA

Stanford University and Weizmann Institute of Science

**SOCIETY for INDUSTRIAL and
APPLIED MATHEMATICS • 1980**

PHILADELPHIA, PENNSYLVANIA 19103

Library of Congress Catalog Card Number: 79-93153.

ISBN: 0-89871-164-9.

Printed in England for the Society for Industrial and Applied Mathematics by
J. W. Arrowsmith Ltd., Winterstoke Road, Bristol BS3 2NT, England.

Contents

CONTENTS

Chapter 6
TERMINATION OF PRODUCTION SYSTEMS

Introduction

Techniques derived from mathematical logic have been applied to many aspects of the programming process. The following lecture notes deal with six of these aspects:

* *partial correctness of programs*: proving that a given program produces the intended results whenever it halts.

* *termination of programs*: proving that a given program will eventually halt.

* *total correctness of programs*: proving both that a given program is partially correct and that it terminates.

* *systematic program annotation*: describing the intermediate behavior of a given program.

* *synthesis of programs*: constructing a program to meet given specifications.

* *termination of production systems*: proving that a system of rewriting rules always halts.

CHAPTER 1

Partial Correctness

We use the following conventions:

Let P be a program;

$\bar{x}$ be all the variables in P;

$\bar{x}_0$ be the initial values of $\bar{x}$ (when computation starts);

$\bar{x}_h$ be the final values of $\bar{x}$ (upon termination of computation).

Let $L_0, L_1, \ldots, L_h$ be a designated set of labels (cutpoints) in P, where L_0 is the entrance and L_h is the exit. (It is assumed that each loop passes through at least one of the designated labels.) A path α between L_i and L_j

is said to be *basic* if there are no designated labels between L_i and L_j.

Let $t_\alpha(\bar{x})$ be the condition for path α to be traversed;

$g_\alpha(\bar{x})$ be a function expressing the change in values along path α:

Thus

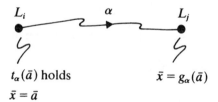

$$t_\alpha(\bar{a}) \text{ holds} \qquad \bar{x} = g_\alpha(\bar{a})$$
$$\bar{x} = \bar{a}$$

Let $\Phi(\bar{x}_0)$ be an *input specification*, giving the range of legal initial values; $\Psi(\bar{x}_0, \bar{x}_h)$ be an *output specification*, giving the desired relation between the initial and final values of $\bar{x}$. We define the following:

P is *partially correct* w.r.t. (with respect to) Φ and Ψ: for every $\bar{x}_0$ such that $\Phi(\bar{x}_0)$ holds, if computation reaches the exit L_h then $\Psi(\bar{x}_0, \bar{x}_h)$ holds.

P *terminates* w.r.t. Φ: for every $\bar{x}_0$ such that $\Phi(\bar{x}_0)$ holds, the computation reaches the exit L_h.

P is *totally correct* w.r.t. Φ and Ψ: P is partially correct w.r.t. Φ and Ψ and P terminates w.r.t. Φ.

A. Invariant method (Floyd (1967), Hoare (1969)). To prove the *partial correctness* of P w.r.t. Φ and Ψ, find a set of predicates $q_0(\bar{x}_0, \bar{x})$, $q_1(\bar{x}_0, \bar{x}), \cdots, q_h(\bar{x}_0, \bar{x})$, corresponding to the labels $L_0, L_1, \cdots, L_h$, such that the following *verification conditions* are satisfied for all $\bar{x}$, $\bar{x}_0$, and $\bar{x}_h$ (universally quantified):

(I1) $\Phi(\bar{x}_0) \Rightarrow q_0(\bar{x}_0, \bar{x}_0)$ (the input specification implies the initial predicate),

(I2) $q_h(\bar{x}_0, \bar{x}_h) \Rightarrow \Psi(\bar{x}_0, \bar{x}_h)$ (the final predicate implies the output specification),

and for each basic path α from L_i to L_j

(I3) $t_\alpha(\bar{x})$ and $q_i(\bar{x}_0, \bar{x}) \Rightarrow q_j(\bar{x}_0, g_\alpha(\bar{x}))$ (the predicate before the path implies the predicate after, whenever the path can be taken).

Verification conditions (I1) and (I3) imply that for each i, $q_i(\bar{x}_0, \bar{x})$ is an *invariant assertion* at L_i, i.e., each time we pass through L_i, $q_i(\bar{x}_0, \bar{x})$ is true for the initial value $\bar{x}_0$ and for the current value of $\bar{x}$. In particular, $q_h(\bar{x}_0, \bar{x})$ is an invariant assertion at L_h, which, by verification condition (I2), implies the partial correctness of the program.

In practice, we usually take $q_0(\bar{x}_0, \bar{x}_0)$ to be $\Phi(\bar{x}_0)$ and $q_h(\bar{x}_0, \bar{x})$ to be $\Psi(\bar{x}_0, \bar{x})$. Then, (I1) and (I2) are guaranteed to hold.

Example: integer square-root program. The following program computes $b = \lfloor \sqrt{a} \rfloor$ for every nonnegative integer a; that is, the final value of b is the largest integer k such that $k \le \sqrt{a}$, i.e., $b^2 \le a < (b+1)^2$.

$$\textbf{input } (a)$$
$$L_0:\ (b, c, d) \leftarrow (0, 1, 1)$$
$$L_1:\ \textbf{if } c > a \textbf{ then } L_h:\ \text{output } (b)$$
$$\textbf{else } (b, d) \leftarrow (b+1, d+2)$$
$$c \leftarrow c + d$$
$$\textbf{goto } L_1.$$

(Note that the value of a is unchanged by the program and that b, c, and d have undefined values at L_0.)

To prove partial correctness w.r.t.

$$\Phi(a_0):\ a_0 \ge 0,$$
$$\Psi(a_0, b_h):\ b_h^2 \le a_0 < (b_h + 1)^2,$$

let

$$q_0(a_0) \text{ be } \Phi(a_0)$$
$$q_h(a_0, b) \text{ be } \Psi(a_0, b),$$

and find a predicate $q_1(a_0, a, b, c, d)$ such that the following (I3) verification conditions hold for all a_0, a, b, c, and d:

$$\Phi(a_0) \Rightarrow q_1(a_0, a_0, 0, 1, 1);$$
$$c > a \text{ and } q_1(a_0, a, b, c, d) \Rightarrow \Psi(a_0, b);$$
$$c \le a \text{ and } q_1(a_0, a, b, c, d) \Rightarrow q_1(a_0, a, b+1, c+d+2, d+2).$$

The invariant assertion

$q_1(a_0, a, b, c, d)$: $a = a_0$ and $b^2 \leqq a$ and $c = (b+1)^2$ and $d = 2b+1$

will do. □

The verification of a program with respect to given input-output specifications consists of three phases: finding appropriate invariant assertions, generating the corresponding verification conditions, and proving that the verification conditions are true. Finding the invariant assertions requires a deep understanding of the principles behind the program, and we therefore assume at this stage that they are provided by the programmer. Thus, the *verification process* can be summarized as follows:

> *program*
> + *input/output specifications*
> + *invariant assertions*

$\downarrow$ *verification-conditions generation*

verification conditions

$\downarrow$ *theorem proving*

yes, no, or don't know.

B. Subgoal method (Manna (1971), Morris and Wegbreit (1977)). This method is also used for proving the partial correctness of programs, but there are two basic differences between the invariant method and the subgoal method: (1) An invariant assertion $q_i(\bar{x}_0, \bar{x})$ relates the current value of $\bar{x}$ to the initial value $\bar{x}_0$. A subgoal assertion $q_i^*(\bar{x}, \bar{x}_h)$ relates current value of $\bar{x}$ to the final value $\bar{x}_h$. Thus $q_i(\bar{x}_0, \bar{x})$ describes what was done so far, while $q_i^*(\bar{x}, \bar{x}_h)$ describes what remains to be done. (2) The invariant method uses forward induction from L_0 to L_h:

$$q_0(\bar{x}_0, \bar{x}_0)$$

$$q_i(\bar{x}_0, \bar{x}) \Rightarrow q_j(\bar{x}_0, g_\alpha(\bar{x})),$$

while the subgoal method uses backward induction from L_h to L_0:

$$q_h^*(\bar{x}_h, \bar{x}_h)$$

$$q_j^*(g_\alpha(\bar{x}), \bar{x}_h) \Rightarrow q_i^*(\bar{x}, \bar{x}_h).$$

To prove the *partial correctness* of P w.r.t. Φ and Ψ by the subgoal method, find a set of predicates $q_0^*(\bar{x}, \bar{x}_h), q_1^*(\bar{x}, \bar{x}_h), \cdots, q_h^*(\bar{x}, \bar{x}_h)$, corresponding to the designated labels $L_0, L_1, \ldots, L_h$, such that the following *verification conditions* are satisfied for all $\bar{x}$, $\bar{x}_0$, and $\bar{x}_h$.

(S1) $q_h^*(\bar{x}_h, \bar{x}_h)$ (the final predicate always holds for the final value of $\bar{x}$),

(S2) $\Phi(x_0)$ and $q_0^*(\bar{x}_0, \bar{x}_h) \Rightarrow \Psi(\bar{x}_0, \bar{x}_h)$ (the input specification and the initial predicate imply the output specification), and for each basic path α from L_i to L_j

(S3) $t_\alpha(\bar{x})$ and $q_j^*(g_\alpha(\bar{x}), \bar{x}_h)$ $\Rightarrow$ $q_i^*(\bar{x}, \bar{x}_h)$ (the predicate after the path implies the predicate before).

Verification conditions (S1) and (S3) imply that for each i, $q_i^*(\bar{x}, \bar{x}_h)$ is a *subgoal assertion* at L_i; i.e., each time we pass through L_i, $q_i^*(\bar{x}, \bar{x}_h)$ is true for the current value of $\bar{x}$ and the final value $\bar{x}_h$. In particular, $q_0^*(\bar{x}, \bar{x}_h)$ is a subgoal assertion at L_0, which, by the verification condition (S2), implies the partial correctness of the program.

In practice, we usually take $q_h^*(\bar{x}, \bar{x}_h)$ to be $\bar{x} = \bar{x}_h$.

Example: *greatest-common divisor program*. The following program computes the greatest-common divisor of two positive integers a_0 and b_0.

$$\text{input } (a_0, b_0)$$
$$L_0: (a, b) \leftarrow (a_0, b_0)$$
$$L_1: \textbf{if } a = 0$$
$$\textbf{then } L_2: \textbf{output } (b)$$
$$\textbf{else } (a, b) \leftarrow (rem\,(b, a), a)$$
$$\textbf{goto } L_1,$$

where $rem\,(b, a)$ stands for the remainder of dividing b by a.

Let

$$\Phi(a_0, b_0): \quad a_0 > 0 \quad \text{and} \quad b_0 > 0,$$

$$\Psi(a_0, b_0, b_h): \quad b_h = gcd\,(a_0, b_0).$$

To prove partial correctness w.r.t. Φ and Ψ by the invariant method, take the invariant assertions:

$q_0(a_0, b_0, a, b): \quad a_0 > 0 \quad \text{and} \quad b_0 > 0, \quad \text{i.e., } \Phi(a_0, b_0),$

$q_1(a_0, b_0, a, b): \quad a \geq 0 \quad \text{and} \quad b > 0 \quad \text{and} \quad gcd\,(a, b) = gcd\,(a_0, b_0),$

$q_2(a_0, b_0, a, b): \quad b = gcd\,(a_0, b_0), \quad \text{i.e., } \Psi(a_0, b_0, b),$

and use the corresponding verifications conditions (I1), (I2), and (I3). Here, $q_i(a_0, b_0, a, b)$ relates the program variables a and b with their initial values a_0, b_0.

To prove partial correctness w.r.t. Φ and Ψ by the subgoal method, take the subgoal assertions:

$q_0^*(a, b, b_h): \quad a \geq 0 \quad \text{and} \quad b > 0 \quad \Rightarrow \quad b_h = gcd\,(a, b),$

$q_1^*(a, b, b_h): \quad a \geq 0 \quad \text{and} \quad b > 0 \quad \Rightarrow \quad b_h = gcd\,(a, b),$

$q_2^*(a, b, b_h): \quad b = b_h,$

and use the corresponding verification conditions (S1), (S2), and (S3). Here, $q_i^*(a, b, b_h)$ relates the current values of the program variables a and b to the final value b_h of b.

C. Subgoal method versus invariant method.

THEOREM. *Any invariant proof can effectively be transformed into a subgoal proof, and vice-versa.*

Proof. (*invariant proof* $\Rightarrow$ *subgoal proof*). Suppose we have an invariant proof showing that P is partially correct w.r.t. Φ and Ψ, i.e., we have a set of invariant assertions $q_i(\bar{x}_0, \bar{x})$ satisfying (I1), (I2), and (I3).

Let us take

$$q_i^*(\bar{x}, \bar{x}_h) \text{ to be } \forall \bar{y}[q_i(\bar{y}, \bar{x}) \Rightarrow \Psi(\bar{y}, \bar{x}_h)].$$

We have to show that (S1), (S2), and (S3) are satisfied.

(S1)   We must show $q_h^*(\bar{x}_h, \bar{x}_h)$, i.e., $\forall \bar{y}[q_h(\bar{y}, \bar{x}_h) \Rightarrow \Psi(\bar{y}, \bar{x}_h)]$. But this follows from (I2).

(S2)   We must show $\Phi(\bar{x}_0)$ and $q_0^*(\bar{x}_0, \bar{x}_h) \Rightarrow \Psi(\bar{x}_0, \bar{x}_h)$, i.e.,

$\Phi(\bar{x}_0)$ and $\forall \bar{y}[q_0(\bar{y}, \bar{x}_0) \Rightarrow \Psi(\bar{y}, \bar{x}_h)] \Rightarrow \Psi(\bar{x}_0, \bar{x}_h)$.

1. $\Phi(\bar{x}_0)$ is given;
2. $\forall \bar{y}[q_0(\bar{y}, \bar{x}_0) \Rightarrow \Psi(\bar{y}, \bar{x}_h)]$ is given;
3. $q_0(\bar{x}_0, \bar{x}_0)$ holds by 1 and (I1);
4. $\Psi(\bar{x}_0, \bar{x}_h)$ holds by 2 and 3.

(S3)   We must show $t_\alpha(\bar{x})$ and $q_j^*(g_\alpha(\bar{x}), \bar{x}_h) \Rightarrow q_i^*(\bar{x}, \bar{x}_h)$, i.e.,

$t_\alpha(\bar{x})$ and $\forall \bar{y}[q_j(\bar{y}, g_\alpha(\bar{x})) \Rightarrow \Psi(\bar{y}, \bar{x}_h)] \Rightarrow \forall \bar{y}[q_i(\bar{y}, \bar{x}) \Rightarrow \Psi(\bar{y}, \bar{x}_h)]$.

1. $t_\alpha(\bar{x})$ is given;
2. $\forall \bar{y}[q_j(\bar{y}, g_\alpha(\bar{x})) \Rightarrow \Psi(\bar{y}, \bar{x}_h)]$ is given;
3. $q_i(\bar{y}, \bar{x})$ holds by assumption;
4. $q_j(\bar{y}, g_\alpha(\bar{x}))$ holds by 1, 3 and (I3)
5. $\Psi(\bar{y}, \bar{x}_h)$ holds by 2 and 4.

(*subgoal proof* $\Rightarrow$ *invariant proof*). Suppose we have a subgoal proof showing that P is partially correct w.r.t. Φ and Ψ, i.e., we have a set of subgoal assertions $q_0^*(\bar{x}, \bar{x}_h), q_1^*(\bar{x}, \bar{x}_h), \cdots, q_h^*(\bar{x}, \bar{x}_h)$ satisfying (S1), (S2), and (S3).

Let us take $q_i(\bar{x}_0, \bar{x})$ to be $\forall \bar{y}[q_i^*(\bar{x}, \bar{y}) \Rightarrow \Psi(\bar{x}_0, \bar{y})]$, and show that (I1), (I2), and (I3) are satisfied.

(I1)   We must show $\Phi(\bar{x}_0) \Rightarrow q_0(\bar{x}_0, \bar{x}_0)$, i.e.,

$\Phi(\bar{x}_0) \Rightarrow \forall \bar{y}[q_0^*(\bar{x}_0, \bar{y}) \Rightarrow \Psi(\bar{x}_0, \bar{y})]$.

1. $\Phi(\bar{x}_0)$ is given;
2. $q_0^*(\bar{x}_0, \bar{y})$ holds by assumption;
3. $\Psi(\bar{x}_0, \bar{y})$ holds by 1, 2, and (S2).

(I2)   We must show $q_h(\bar{x}_0, \bar{x}_h) \Rightarrow \Psi(\bar{x}_0, \bar{x}_h)$, i.e.,

$\forall \bar{y}[q_h^*(\bar{x}_h, \bar{y}) \Rightarrow \Psi(\bar{x}_0, \bar{y})] \Rightarrow \Psi(\bar{x}_0, \bar{x}_h)$.

1. $\forall \bar{y}[q_h^*(\bar{x}_h, \bar{y}) \Rightarrow \Psi(\bar{x}_0, \bar{y})]$ is given;
2. $q_h^*(\bar{x}_h, \bar{x}_h)$ holds by (S1);
3. $\Psi(\bar{x}_0, \bar{x}_h)$ holds by 1 and 2.

(I3)   We must show $t_\alpha(\bar{x})$ and $q_i(\bar{x}_0, \bar{x}) \Rightarrow q_j(\bar{x}_0, g_\alpha(\bar{x}))$, i.e.,

$t_\alpha(\bar{x})$ and $\forall \bar{y}[q_i^*(\bar{x}, \bar{y}) \Rightarrow \Psi(\bar{x}_0, \bar{y})] \Rightarrow \forall \bar{y}[q_j^*(g_\alpha(\bar{x}), \bar{y}) \Rightarrow \Psi(\bar{x}_0, \bar{y})]$.

1. $t_\alpha(\bar{x})$ is given;
2. $\forall \bar{y}[q_i^*(\bar{x}, \bar{y}) \Rightarrow \Psi(\bar{x}_0, \bar{y})]$ is given;
3. $q_j^*(g_\alpha(\bar{x}), \bar{y})$ holds by assumption;
4. $q_i^*(\bar{x}, \bar{y})$ holds by 1, 3 and (S3)
5. $\Psi(\bar{x}_0, \bar{y})$ holds by 2 and 4. $\square$

CHAPTER 2

Termination

A. Well-founded ordering method (Floyd (1967)).

DEFINITION. A *well-founded set* $(W, >)$ consists of a nonempty set W and a strict partial ordering $>$ on W, that has no infinite decreasing sequences.

That is, $>$ is a transitive, asymmetric, and irreflexive binary relation on W such that for no infinite sequence $a_0, a_1, a_2, \cdots$ of elements of W do we have $a_0 > a_1 > a_2 > \cdots$.

Note that there may exist distinct elements a and b such that neither $a > b$ nor $b > a$. The set of nonnegative integers N with the regular $>$ ordering, i.e. $(N, >)$, is well-founded; but the set of all integers Z with the same ordering, i.e. $(Z, >)$, is not well-founded.

To prove the termination of program P w.r.t. $\Phi(\bar{x}_0)$:

(1) Find a set of predicates $q_0(\bar{x}_0, \bar{x}), q_1(\bar{x}_0, \bar{x}), \cdots, q_{h-1}(\bar{x}_0, \bar{x})$, associated with the designated labels $L_0, L_1, \cdots, L_{h-1}$, such that for every $\bar{x}_0$ and $\bar{x}$:

    (W1) $\Phi(\bar{x}_0) \Rightarrow q_0(\bar{x}_0, \bar{x}_0)$ (the input specification implies the initial predicate), and

    (W2) $t_\alpha(\bar{x})$ and $q_i(\bar{x}_0, \bar{x}) \Rightarrow q_j(\bar{x}_0, g_\alpha(\bar{x}))$ for every basic path α from L_i to L_j (the predicate before the path implies the predicate after).

(2) Find a well-founded set $(W, >)$ and a set of expressions $e_1(\bar{x}_0, \bar{x}), \cdots, e_{h-1}(\bar{x}_0, \bar{x})$, called *termination functions*, such that

    (W3) $q_i(\bar{x}_0, \bar{x}) \Rightarrow e_i(\bar{x}_0, \bar{x}) \in W$ for each label L_i that is on some loop (the value of the expression belongs to W when control passes through L_i), and

    (W4) $t_\alpha(\bar{x})$ and $q_i(\bar{x}_0, \bar{x}) \Rightarrow e_i(\bar{x}_0, \bar{x}) > e_j(\bar{x}_0, g_\alpha(\bar{x}))$ for every basic path α from L_i to L_j which is on some loop (as control passes from L_i to L_j, the value of the corresponding expression is reduced).

Note that (W1) and (W2) imply that each $q_i(\bar{x}_0, \bar{x})$ is an invariant assertion at L_i; it is used in (W3) and (W4) to restrict the domain of e_i.

Termination conditions (W1) to (W4) imply the termination of the program. For, suppose the program does not terminate for some $\bar{x}_0$, such that $\Phi(\bar{x}_0)$. Then the computation for $\bar{x}_0$ passes through an infinite sequence of labels

$$L_{i_1}, L_{i_2}, \cdots.$$

The corresponding values of $\bar{x}$ are

$$\bar{x}_{i_1}, \bar{x}_{i_2}, \cdots.$$

Then by (W1) and (W2)

$$q_{i_1}(\bar{x}_0, \bar{x}_{i_1}), q_{i_2}(\bar{x}_0, \bar{x}_{i_2}), \cdots$$

9

hold, and by (W3) and (W4)

$$e_{i_1}(\bar{x}_0, \bar{x}_{i_1}) > e_{i_2}(\bar{x}_0, \bar{x}_{i_2}) > \cdots.$$

We have obtained an infinite decreasing sequence of elements of W, which contradicts the well-foundedness of W.

Example: *integer square-root program*. Let us consider again

> **input** (a)
> L_0: $(b, c, d) \leftarrow (0, 1, 1)$
> L_1: **if** $c > a$ **then** L_2: **output** (b)
> > **else** $(b, d) \leftarrow (b + 1, d + 2)$
> > $c \leftarrow c + d$
> > **goto** L_1.

To prove termination of the program w.r.t. $a_0 \geqq 0$, take $q_0(a_0)$ to be $a_0 \geqq 0$, $q_1(a_0, a, b, c, d)$ to be $a = a_0$ and $c - d \leqq a$ and $d > 0$, and show

(W1) $a_0 \geqq 0$ $\Rightarrow$ $a_0 \geqq 0$
(W2) $a_0 \geqq 0$ $\Rightarrow$ $q_1(a_0, a_0, 0, 1, 1)$,
         $c \leqq a$ and $q_1(a_0, a, b, c, d)$ $\Rightarrow$ $q_1(a_0, a, b + 1, c + d + 2, d + 2)$.

Take $(W, >)$ to be $(N, >)$, $e_1(a_0, a, b, c, d)$ to be $a - c + d$, and show

(W3) $q_1(a_0, a, b, c, d)$ $\Rightarrow$ $a - c + d \geqq 0$;
(W4) $c \leqq a$ and $q_1(a_0, a, b, c, d)$ $\Rightarrow$ $a - c + d > a - (c + d + 2) + (d + 2)$.   □

B. The multiset ordering (Dershowitz and Manna (1979)). Let us consider a special case of well-founded ordering that is particularly useful for termination proofs.

A *multiset*, or *bag*, over N is a "set" of natural numbers with multiple occurrences allowed. For example, $\{4, 2, 2, 2, 0, 0\}$ is a multiset over N. The set of all *finite* multisets over N is denoted by $\mathcal{M}(N)$.

Under the *multiset ordering*, $M \gg M'$, where $M, M' \in \mathcal{M}(N)$, if M' may be obtained from M by the removal of at least one element from M and/or the replacement of at least one element in M with any *finite* number of smaller elements. Thus

$$\{4, 2, 2, 2, 0, 0\}$$
$$\vee$$
$$\vee \qquad\qquad 2, 0, 0 \text{ is removed.}$$
$$\{4, 2, 2\}$$
$$\vee$$
$$\vee \qquad\qquad 2 \text{ is replaced by } 1, 1, 1, 0, 0.$$
$$\{4, 2, 1, 1, 1, 0, 0\}$$
$$\vee \qquad\qquad 4 \text{ is replaced by } 3, 3, 2, 2$$
$$\vee \qquad\qquad \text{and } 1, 1, 1, 0, 0 \text{ are removed}$$
$$\{3, 3, 2, 2, 2\}.$$

Since $(\mathcal{M}(N), \gg)$ can be shown to be a well-founded set, it can be used for proving the termination of programs.

Example: *shunting yard program*. Consider the program

> **loop** until the shunting yard is empty
> select a train
> **if** the train consists of a single car
>   **then** remove it (from the yard)
>   **else** split it into two shorter trains
> **repeat**

This program (due to Dijkstra) is nondeterministic, since "select" and "split" are not uniquely determined.

Let *trains*(*yard*) be the number of trains in the yard, *cars*(*yard*) be the total number of cars in the yard, and for any *train* ∈ *yard* let *cars*(*train*) be the number of cars it contains. We present two proofs of termination.

A regular termination proof uses the

> well-founded set: $(N, >)$
> termination function: $2 \cdot cars(yard) - trains(yard)$.

Each iteration of the program loop clearly reduces the value of the termination function: removing a one-car train from the yard decreases $2 \cdot cars(yard)$ by 2, and increases $-trains(yard)$ by 1, thereby decreasing the termination function by 1; splitting a train conserves the number of cars in the yard and increases the number of trains in the yard by 1, thereby decreasing the value of the termination function by 1.

The multiset termination proof uses the

> well-founded set: $(\mathcal{M}(N), \gg)$
> termination function: $\{cars(train): train \in yard\}$.

Each iteration of the program loop decreases the value of the termination function under the multiset ordering: removing a train from the yard reduces the multiset by removing one element; splitting a train replaces one element with two smaller ones, corresponding to the two shorter trains. □

In general, a *multiset over S* is a "set" allowing multiple occurrences of elements of *S*. The set of all *finite* multisets over *S* is denoted by $\mathcal{M}(S)$.

For a given partially-ordered set $(S, >)$, the *multiset ordering* $\gg$ between multisets over *S* is defined as follows:

$$M \gg M', \quad \text{where } M, M' \in \mathcal{M}(S),$$

if for some $X, Y, Z \in \mathcal{M}(S)$, X not empty,

$$M = X \cup Z \quad \text{and} \quad M' = Y \cup Z$$

and

$$(\forall y \in Y)(\exists x \in X)\, x > y$$

(where $\cup$ denotes multiset union). In words, a multiset is reduced by the removal of one or more elements (those in X) and their replacement with any finite number—possibly zero—of elements (those in Y), each of which is smaller than one of the elements that have been removed.

THEOREM. $(\mathcal{M}(S), \gg)$ *is well founded* $\Leftrightarrow$ $(S, >)$ *is well founded.*

Example: *tips program*. Let $tips(t)$ = the number of tips (terminal nodes) of a full binary tree t; *tips* is defined recursively by

$$tips(t) \;\Leftarrow\; \textbf{if } t \text{ is a tip}$$
$$\textbf{then } 1$$
$$\textbf{else } tips(left(t)) + tips(right(t));$$

e.g.,

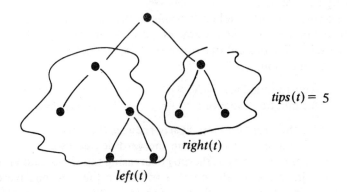

$$tips(t) = 5$$

$$right(t)$$

$$left(t)$$

Let us consider the iterative program for computing $tips(t_0)$

```
          input (t₀)
    L₀: S ← (t₀)
        C ← 0
    L₁: if S = ( )
        then L₂: output (C)
        else y ← head(S)
             S ← tail(S)
             if y is a tip
             then C ← C + 1
                  goto L₁
             else S ← left(y) · right(y) · S
                  goto L₁.
```

This program initially inserts the given tree t_0 as a single element of the stack S of trees. With each iteration, the first element is removed from the stack. If it is a tip, the element is counted; otherwise, its left and right subtrees are inserted as the first and second elements of the stack. The process terminates when the stack is empty; the counter C is then the number of tips in the given tree.

Regular termination proof: Take

$$(N, >), \qquad e_1(S) = \sum_{s \in S} nodes(s),$$

or

$(N \times N, >)$ where $>$ is the lexicographic ordering
                     between pairs of nonnegative integers and

$$e_1(S) = \left(\sum_{s \in S} tips(s), \, tips(head(S)) \right).$$

Multiset-ordering proof: Since in each iteration $head(S)$ is either removed or replaced by two smaller subtrees, take

$$(\mathcal{M}(N), \gg), \quad e_1(S) = \{nodes(s): s \in S\} \qquad \text{or}$$

$$(\mathcal{M}(N), \gg), \quad e_1(S) = \{tips(s): s \in S\} \qquad \text{or}$$

$(\mathcal{M}(T), \gg)$ where T is the set of all full binary trees
                  and $>$ is the subtree ordering
$e_1(S) = \{s : s \in S\}$.   □

Example: *Ackerman's program.* Ackerman's function $a(m, n)$ over the nonnegative integers is defined recursively as follows:

$$a(m, n) \quad \Leftarrow \quad \textbf{if } m = 0 \textbf{ then } n + 1$$
$$\textbf{else if } n = 0 \textbf{ then } a(m - 1, 1)$$
$$\textbf{else } a(m - 1, a(m, n - 1)).$$

The following is an iterative program to compute the function:

```
S ← (m)
z ← n
loop L₁: assert a(m, n) = a(s_|S|, a(s_|S|-1, · · · , a(s_2, a(s_1, z)) · · · ))
         if s_1 = 0 then S ← (s_|S|, · · · , s_2)
                         z ← z + 1
         else
         if z = 0 then S ← (s_|S|, · · · , s_2, s_1 - 1)
                       z ← 1
                  else S ← (s_|S|, · · · , s_2, s_1 - 1, s_1)
                       z ← z - 1
         until S = ( )
         repeat
assert z = a(m, n),
```

where $|S|$ denotes the number of elements in the stack S.

To prove termination of this program, consider the set $(N \times N, >)$ of lexicographically-ordered pairs of natural numbers, and use the corresponding multiset ordering over $N \times N$, i.e., $(\mathcal{M}(N \times N), \gg)$. Take

$$e_1(S, z): \quad \{(s_{|S|} + 1, 0), (s_{|S|-1} + 1, 0), \cdots, (s_2 + 1, 0), (s_1, z)\}$$

$$q_1(S, z): \quad S \neq ( ) \quad \text{and} \quad z \geq 0 \quad \text{and} \quad \forall i (1 \leq i \leq |S| \Rightarrow s_i \geq 0).$$

The proof considers the three cases, corresponding to the three branches of the
conditional in the loop:

(1) *Case $s_1 = 0$:*

$$\{(s_{|S|}+1, 0), \cdots, (s_3+1, 0), (s_2+1, 0), (s_1, z)\}$$

$$\Downarrow$$

$$\{(s_{|S|}+1, 0), \cdots, (s_3+1, 0), (s_2, z+1)\},$$

since $(s_2+1, 0) > (s_2, z+1)$ and (s_1, z) has been removed.

(2) *Case $s_1 = 0$ and $z = 0$:*

$$\{(s_{|S|}+1, 0), \cdots, (s_2+1, 0), (s_1, z)\}$$

$$\Downarrow$$

$$\{(s_{|S|}+1, 0), \cdots, (s_2+1, 0), (s_1-1, 1)\},$$

since $(s_1, z) > (s_1-1, 1)$.

(3) *Case $s_1 \neq 0$ and $z \neq 0$:*

$$\{(s_{|S|}+1, 0), \cdots, (s_2+1, 0), (s_1, z)\}$$

$$\Downarrow$$

$$\{(s_{|S|}+1, 0), \cdots, (s_2+1, 0), (s_1, 0), (s_1, z-1)\},$$

since $(s_1, z) > (s_1, 0)$ and $(s_1, z) > (s_1, z-1)$. $\square$

CHAPTER 3

Total Correctness

A. Intermittent method (Burstall (1974), Manna and Waldinger (1978)). The two main characteristics of this method are the following: (1) We prove total correctness, i.e., partial correctness and termination, w.r.t. $\Phi(\bar{x}_0)$ and $\Psi(\bar{x}_0, \bar{x}_h)$ in a single proof. (2) An invariant assertion means

$$\text{always} \quad q_i(\bar{x}_0, \bar{x}) \text{ at } L_i ;$$

a subgoal assertion means

$$\text{always} \quad q_i^*(\bar{x}, \bar{x}_h) \text{ at } L_i ;$$

while an intermittent assertion means

$$\text{sometimes} \quad Q_i(\bar{x}_0, \bar{x}) \text{ at } L_i.$$

That is, sometime (eventually) control will pass through L_i and satisfy $Q_i(\bar{x}_0, \bar{x})$ for the current value of $\bar{x}$ and the initial value $\bar{x}_0$. Thus, control may pass through L_i many times without satisfying Q_i, but control must pass through L_i at least once with $Q_i(\bar{x}_0, \bar{x})$ true.

Example: *tips program*. Let us consider again the iterative program for computing the number of tips (terminal nodes) of a full binary tree.

$$
\begin{aligned}
&\textbf{input } (t_0)\\
L_0\colon\ &S \leftarrow (t_0)\\
&C \leftarrow 0\\
L_1\colon\ &\textbf{if } S = (\ )\\
&\quad \textbf{then } L_2\colon \textbf{output } (C)\\
&\quad \textbf{else } \ y \leftarrow head(S)\\
&\qquad\quad S \leftarrow tail(S)\\
&\qquad\quad \textbf{if } y \text{ is a tip}\\
&\qquad\quad \textbf{then } C \leftarrow C + 1\\
&\qquad\quad \textbf{goto } L_1\\
&\qquad \textbf{else } \ S \leftarrow left(y) \cdot right(y) \cdot S\\
&\qquad\quad\ \textbf{goto } L_1.
\end{aligned}
$$

We can express the total correctness of this program as the following:
THEOREM.

$$
\begin{aligned}
&\text{if (sometime) at } L_0\\
&\text{then sometime } C = \text{tips } (t_0) \text{ at } L_2.
\end{aligned}
$$

15

This theorem states the termination of the program in addition to its partial correctness, because it implies that control must eventually reach the program's exit L_2 and satisfy the output specification.

To prove the total correctness of the program we must supply a lemma describing the behavior of the loop using an intermittent assertion at L_1.

LEMMA.

$$\text{if sometime} \quad C = c \text{ and } S = t \cdot s \text{ at } L_1$$
$$\text{then sometime} \quad C = c + \text{tips}(t) \text{ and } S = s \text{ at } L_1.$$

That is, if we enter the loop with some subtree t at the head of the stack, then eventually the tips of t will be counted and t will be removed from the stack. *Note that we may need to return to L_1 many times before the tips of t are counted.*

Proof of Theorem. (*Lemma* $\Rightarrow$ *Theorem.*) Suppose

$$\text{sometime} \quad \text{at } L_0.$$

By computation

$$\text{sometime} \quad C = 0 \text{ and } S = (t_0) = t_0 \cdot (\ ) \text{ at } L_1.$$

By the lemma

$$\text{sometime} \quad C = 0 + tips(t_0) \text{ and } S = (\ ) \text{ at } L_1.$$

By computation

$$\text{sometime} \quad C = tips(t_0) \text{ at } L_2.$$

Proof of Lemma. Proof is by *complete induction* on the structure of $head(S) = t$. Assume the lemma holds whenever $head(S) = t'$ where t' is any subtree of t. Suppose

$$\text{sometime} \quad C = c \text{ and } S = t \cdot s \text{ at } L_1.$$

Case t is a tip: By computation,

$$\text{sometime} \quad C = c + 1 \text{ and } S = s \text{ at } L_1,$$

i.e., by the definition of *tips*,

$$\text{sometime} \quad C = c + tips(t) \text{ and } S = s \text{ at } L_1.$$

Case t is not a tip: By computation,

$$\text{sometime} \quad C = c \text{ and } S = left(t) \cdot right(t) \cdot s \text{ at } L_1.$$

By induction hypothesis with $t' = left(t)$,

$$\text{sometime} \quad C = c + tips(left(t)) \text{ and } S = right(t) \cdot s \text{ at } L_1.$$

By induction hypothesis with $t' = right(t)$,

$$\text{sometime} \quad C = c + tips(left(t)) + tips(right(t)) \text{ and } S = s \text{ at } L_1,$$

i.e., by the definition of *tips*

$$\text{sometime} \quad C = c + tips(t) \text{ and } S = s \text{ at } L_1. \quad \square$$

Note that once the lemma was formulated (this required some ingenuity) and the basis for the induction decided, the proofs proceeded in a fairly mechanical manner. An invariant proof of the partial correctness of the program will use the invariant assertion

$$q_1(t, C, S): tips(t) = C + \sum_{s \in S} tips(s) \quad \text{at } L_1.$$

The intermittent method allows us to relate the point at which we are about to count the tips of a subtree t to the point at which we have completed the counting and to consider the many executions of the body of the loop between these points as a single unit, which corresponds naturally to a single recursive call $tips(t)$. On the other hand, the invariant method requires that we identify a condition that relates the situation before and after *each single* execution of the body of the loop.

The intermittent method is as powerful as any one of the other methods in the following sense:

THEOREM. *There exist effective procedures for the following transformation of proofs*:

(a) *Invariant proof* $\Rightarrow$ *Intermittent proof (assuming termination)*;

(b) *Subgoal proof* $\Rightarrow$ *Intermittent proof (assuming termination)*;

(c) *Well-founded ordering proof* $\Rightarrow$ *Intermittent proof*.

In other words, each proof by one of the conventional methods can be translated into an intermittent proof. The translation process is purely mechanical and does not increase the complexity of the original proof.

Is it possible that a similar translation could be performed in the other direction? We believe not. We have seen no invariant proof for the *tips* program that does not require consideration of the sum of the tips of *all* the elements in the stack. To make such an argument rigorously, we would have to formulate a precise notion of "complexity of proofs."

Application: correctness of continuously operating programs. So far we have considered only programs that are expected to terminate, and proved their behavior (correctness) when they terminate. Some programs, such as operating systems, airline-reservation systems, and management information systems are never expected to terminate—they are *continuously operating programs.* The correctness of such programs cannot be expressed by output specifications, but rather their intended behavior while running must be specified. The specification often involves stating that *some event A is inevitably followed by some other event B.* Such a relationship connects two different states of the program and, generally, cannot be phrased as an invariant assertion. In other words, the standard tools for proving correctness of terminating programs are not appropriate for continuously operating programs. The intermittent method is a natural approach here.

Let us consider the following sequential "operating system":

$$L_0: \textbf{read}(requests)$$
$$L_1: \textbf{if } requests = (\ )$$
$$\qquad \textbf{then goto } L_0$$
$$\qquad\qquad \textbf{else } job \leftarrow head(requests)$$
$$\qquad\qquad requests \leftarrow tail(requests)$$
$$\qquad L_2: \quad process(job)$$
$$\qquad\qquad \textbf{goto } L_1.$$

At each iteration, the program reads a list *requests* of jobs to be processed. If *requests* is empty, the program will continue reading indefinitely until a nonempty *requests* list is read. The system will then process the jobs one by one; when they are all processed, the system will again read a *requests* list.

The correctness of this program can be expressed as

if sometime $j \in requests$ at L_1 then sometime $job = j$ at L_2,

i.e., if a job is read into the *requests* list, it will eventually be processed. (It is assumed that *process* itself terminates.)

CHAPTER 4

Systematic Program Annotation

(Dershowitz and Manna (1977)).

The invariant method for proving the partial correctness of programs requires that the program be annotated with intermediate invariant assertions. Normally, it is expected that these invariants are to be supplied by the programmer. Let us examine, in the context of a particular example, to what extent we can expect this to be done automatically.

We are given a real-division program that is supposed to approximate the quotient c/d of two real numbers c and d, where $0 \leqq c < d$, within tolerance $e > 0$:

Input specification: $0 \leqq c < d$ and $0 < e$.

Output specification: $q \leqq c/d$ and $c/d < q + e$.

The program is

P: **begin**
☞ B: **assert** $0 \leqq c < d$ and $0 < e$
    $(q, qq, r, rr) \leftarrow (0, 0, 1, d)$
    loop L:
        until $r \leqq e$
        if $qq + rr \leqq c$ **then** $(q, qq) \leftarrow (q + r, qq + rr)$
        $(r, rr) \leftarrow (r/2, rr/2)$
        repeat
☞ E: **suggest** $q \leqq c/d$ and $c/d < q + e$
    end.

Our goal is to *document* the program in a systematic way, expressing the behavior of the program. If the program is correct, prove correctness; if the program is incorrect, debug it.

We distinguish between three types of invariants:

1. *Global invariants*: "**assert** α in P"—relation α holds at all places (labels) and at all times during the execution of program segment P.

2. *Local invariants*: "**assert** α at L" or "L: **assert** α"—relation α holds each time control is at label L.

3. *Candidates for invariants*: "**suggest** α at L" or "L: **suggest** α"—relation α is believed to be invariant at L, but is not yet verified.

Examples. (1) $0 \leqq c < d$ and $0 < e$ are global invariants, since c, d and e are not changed in the real-division program P.

(2) $q \leqq c/d$ and $c/d < q + e$ are candidates for invariants at E, since we hope but are not sure that the given program is correct.

19

A. Range of individual variables. We derive global invariants by considering only assignment statements.

(i) $r \leftarrow 1$ or $r \leftarrow r/2$ in P; therefore

$$(1) \quad \textbf{assert} \ (\exists n \in N) \ r = 1/2^n \quad \text{in } P$$

One can then deduce the global invariant $0 < r \leq 1$ in P.
$rr \leftarrow d$ or $rr \leftarrow rr/2$ in P; therefore

$$(2) \quad \textbf{assert} \ (\exists n \in N) \ rr = d/2^n \quad \text{in } P$$

One can deduce the global invariant $0 < rr \leq d$ in P.
(iii) $q \leftarrow 0$ or $q \leftarrow q + r$ in P. Since $(\exists n \in N) \ r = 1/2^n$ by (1), we have

$$(3) \quad \textbf{assert} \ (\exists m, n \in N) \ q = m/2^n \quad \text{in } P$$

(iv) $qq \leftarrow 0$ or $qq \leftarrow qq + rr$ in P. Since $(\exists n \in N) \ rr = d/2^n$ by (2), we have

$$(4) \quad \textbf{assert} \ (\exists m, n \in N) \ qq = d \cdot (m/2^n) \quad \text{in } P$$

B. Relation between variables. Again, we consider only assignment statements and derive global invariants.

(i) $(r, rr) \leftarrow (1, d)$ or $(r, rr) \leftarrow (r/2, rr/2)$; the original proportion between r and rr is preserved, therefore

$$r \cdot d = 1 \cdot rr \quad \text{in } P,$$

or simply

$$(5) \quad \textbf{assert} \ rr = d \cdot r \quad \text{in } P$$

(ii) $(q, qq) \leftarrow (0, 0)$ or $(q, qq) \leftarrow (q + r, qq + rr)$. Since $rr = d \cdot r$ by (5), we have

$$(q, qq) \leftarrow (0, 0) \quad \text{or} \quad (q, qq) \leftarrow (q + r, qq + d \cdot r);$$

thus

$$(6) \quad \textbf{assert} \ qq = d \cdot q \quad \text{in } P$$

C. Control invariants. Analyzing the effect of the exit test $r \leq e$, we get

$$(q, qq, r, rr) \leftarrow (0, 0, 1, d)$$

☞ **assert** $r = 1$
    loop L:
        until $r \leq e$
☞   **assert** $r > e$
        if $qq + rr \leq c$ **then** $(q, qq) \leftarrow (q + r, qq + rr)$
☞   **assert** $r > e$
        $(r, rr) \leftarrow (r/2, rr/2)$
☞   **assert** $2r > e$
        repeat
    assert $r \leq e$.

Thus

$$\boxed{(7) \quad \textbf{assert } r = 1 \text{ or } 2r > e \quad \text{at } L}$$

Analyzing the effect of the conditional test $qq + rr \leq c$, we get

$$(q, qq, r, rr) \leftarrow (0, 0, 1, d)$$

☞ **assert** $(q, qq, r, rr) = (0, 0, 1, d)$
    loop L:
        until $r \leq e$
        if $qq + rr \leq c$ **then assert** $qq + rr \leq c$
                        $(q, qq) \leftarrow (q + r, qq + rr)$
                        assert $qq \leq c$
        else assert $c < qq + rr$
☞   **suggest** $qq \leq c$ and $c < qq + rr$
        $(r, rr) \leftarrow (r/2, rr/2)$
☞   **suggest** $qq \leq c$ and $c < qq + 2rr$
        repeat.

Thus we have

    suggest $(q, qq, r, rr) = (0, 0, 1, d)$ or $qq \leq c$ at L

and

    suggest $(q, qq, r, rr) = (0, 0, 1, d)$ or $c < qq + 2rr$ at L.

In both cases the first disjunct implies the second, i.e.,

$$qq = 0 \quad \Rightarrow \quad qq \leq c \quad \text{and}$$
$$(qq = 0 \text{ and } rr = d) \quad \Rightarrow \quad c < qq + 2rr,$$

and we have therefore

    suggest $qq \leq c$ at L

    suggest $c < qq + 2rr$ at L.

Both candidates can be verified and we get

$$(8) \quad \textbf{assert } qq \leqq c \quad \text{at } L$$

$$(9) \quad \textbf{assert } c < qq + 2rr \quad \text{at } L$$

D. Debugging. We have invariants (1) to (9) at L. Thus we can derive invariants (1) to (9) and $r \leqq e$ at E.

(Note that we have not used the output specification at all.) We can conclude at E:

$$\left. \begin{array}{l} qq = d \cdot q \quad \text{(by (6))} \\ qq \leqq c \quad \text{(by (8))} \end{array} \right\} \quad \Rightarrow \quad q \leqq c/d ;$$

and

$$\left. \begin{array}{l} rr = d \cdot r \quad \text{(by (5))} \\ qq = d \cdot q \quad \text{(by (6))} \\ c < qq + 2rr \quad \text{(by (9))} \\ r \leqq e \end{array} \right\} \quad \Rightarrow \quad c < d \cdot q + 2d \cdot r \quad \Rightarrow \quad c/d < q + 2e.$$

So we have $q \leqq c/d$ as desired, but $c/d < q + 2e$ rather than $c/d < q + e$. To debug the program we have to change $c/d < q + 2e$ to $c/d < q + e$, while preserving $q \leqq c/d$.

This suggests the correction

replace all occurrences of e by $e/2$.

The correct program is accordingly

Note that the output specification is now asserted rather than suggested.

E. Termination and run-time analysis. Let us consider the corrected program augmented with a counter n

$$B: \textbf{assert } 0 \leqq c < d, \ 0 < e$$
$$(q, qq, r, rr) \leftarrow (0, 0, 1, d)$$
☞ $n \leftarrow 0$
$\quad\quad$ **loop** $L: \cdots$
$$\textbf{until } 2r \leqq e$$
$$\textbf{if } qq + rr \leqq c \ \textbf{then } (q, qq) \leftarrow (q + r, qq + rr)$$
$$(r, rr) \leftarrow (r/2, rr/2)$$
☞ $\quad\quad n \leftarrow n + 1$
$\quad\quad$ **repeat.**

We have the following additional global invariants
(i) $n \leftarrow 0$ or $n \leftarrow n + 1$; therefore

$$\boxed{(10) \quad \textbf{assert } n \in N \quad \text{in } P}$$

(ii) $(r, n) \leftarrow (1, 0)$ or $(r, n) \leftarrow (r/2, n + 1)$; therefore

$$\boxed{(11) \quad \textbf{assert } r = 1/2^n \quad \text{in } P}$$

(iii) $(rr, n) \leftarrow (d, 0)$ or $(rr, n) \leftarrow (rr/2, n + 1)$; therefore

$$\boxed{(12) \quad \textbf{assert } rr = d/2^n \quad \text{in } P}$$

We have at E:

$$\left.\begin{array}{l} r = 1/2^n \quad \text{(by (11))} \\ r = 1 \text{ or } 4r > e \quad \text{(by (7))} \\ 2r \leqq e \end{array}\right\} \ \Rightarrow \ 2 \cdot 1/2^n \leqq e \quad \text{and} \quad (1/2^n = 1 \text{ or } 4 \cdot 1/2^n > e)$$

$$\Rightarrow \ 1 - \log_2 e \leqq n \quad \text{and} \quad (n = 0 \text{ or } n < 2 - \log_2 e).$$

Therefore

$\quad\quad\quad 1 - \log_2 e$ is lower bound on n at E;

$\quad\quad\quad 2 - \log_2 e$ is upper bound on n at L $\quad \Rightarrow \quad$ termination.

E. Termination and run-time ...

CHAPTER 5

Synthesis of Programs

(Manna and Waldinger (1979)).

The goal: constructing programs to meet given specifications. The *specification language* consists of high-level constructs that enable us to describe in a very *direct*, *precise*, and *natural* way what is in the user's mind.

For example, a program to find the maximum z of an array of numbers a is specified as follows:

$$max(a, n) \quad \Leftarrow \quad \textbf{achieve} \quad all(a[0:n]) \leqq z$$
$$\text{and } z \in a[0:n] \qquad\qquad\qquad output \ specification$$
$$\text{and only } z \text{ changed}$$
$$\textbf{where} \quad a \text{ is an array of numbers}$$
$$\text{and } n \text{ is an integer} \qquad\qquad input \ specification$$
$$\text{and } 0 \leqq n$$

Our *target language* will be a LISP-like language (if-then-else, recursion) with arrays and assignments. The specification language consists of the target-language constructs (*primitive constructs*) and high-level constructs (*nonprimitive constructs*) that are not in the target language.

A. The weakest precondition operator. Let us consider a program segment of the form

where P and P' are conditions and F is a program segment that always terminates.

(1) $\{P'\} F \{P\}$ means

> if P' is true before executing F,
> then P is true after executing F.

(2) $wp(F, P) = P'$ means

> P' is true before executing F,
> if and only if
> P is true after executing F.

P' is called the *weakest precondition* of F and P.

For example, for the program segment

$$\downarrow - - - ?$$

$$\boxed{x \leftarrow x + 1}$$

$$\downarrow - - - x \geq 1$$

we have

$$\{x \geq 0\}\, x \leftarrow x + 1 \,\{x \geq 1\},$$

$$\{x \geq 1\}\, x \leftarrow x + 1 \,\{x \geq 1\},$$

$$\{x \geq 2\}\, x \leftarrow x + 1 \,\{x \geq 1\},$$

$$\vdots$$

but

$$wp(x \leftarrow x + 1, x \geq 1) = x \geq 0.$$

In general,

$$wp(x \leftarrow t, P(x)) = P(t),$$

because $P(t)$ is true before executing $x \leftarrow t$ if and only if $P(x)$ is true afterwards. We also have

$$wp(\Lambda, P) = P \quad \text{where } \Lambda \text{ is the empty program}$$
$$wp(\textbf{if } q \textbf{ then } S_1 \textbf{ else } S_2, P) = (q \Rightarrow wp(S_1, P))$$
$$\text{and } (\text{not } q \Rightarrow wp(S_2, P))$$
$$wp(\textbf{if } q \textbf{ then } S, P) = (q \Rightarrow wp(S, P))$$
$$\text{and } (\text{not } q \Rightarrow P)$$
$$wp(S_1 S_2, P) = wp(S_1, wp(S_2, P))$$
$$wp(\textbf{achieve } Q, P) = \textit{true} \quad \text{if } Q \Rightarrow P.$$
$$wp(\textit{interchange}(u, v), P(u, v)) = P(v, u).$$

For recursive calls we have the following rule:
Suppose

$$f(x) \Leftarrow B(x) \text{ is the definition of a recursive function } f,$$

$$f(s) \text{ is a recursive call, and}$$

$$> \text{ is a well-founded ordering on the domain of } f.$$

Then

$$P'(s) = wp(f(s), P(s)),$$

if we can prove

$$P'(x) = wp(B(x), P(x))$$

under the inductive assumption

$$P'(t) = wp(f(t), P(t)) \quad \text{for any } t \text{ such that } t < x.$$

B. Transformation rules. The basic tools we use for synthesis are transformation rules. A *transformation rule* is of the form

$$t \quad \Rightarrow \quad t'.$$

It denotes that an expression t, which can be any part of the current program description, may be replaced by an expression t'. A transformation rule can also be of form

$$t \quad \Rightarrow \quad t' \quad \text{if } P$$

which means that the transformation may be applied only if condition P is true.
Here are some transformation rules that will be used in the following example:
(1) *the creation rule*:

$$\textbf{achieve } P \quad \Rightarrow \quad \begin{cases} \textbf{achieve } wp(F, P) \\ F \end{cases} \qquad \text{for any statement } F,$$

e.g. the *assignment-formation rule*:

$$\textbf{achieve } P(x) \quad \Rightarrow \quad \begin{cases} \textbf{achieve } P(t) \\ x \leftarrow t \end{cases} \qquad \text{for any term } t$$

(2) *achieve-elimination rule*:

$$\textbf{achieve } P \quad \Rightarrow \quad \textbf{prove } P$$

(3) *prove-elimination rule*:

$$\textbf{prove } \textit{true} \quad \Rightarrow \quad \Lambda$$

(4) *composition-identity rule*:

$$F\Lambda \quad \Rightarrow \quad F$$
$$\Lambda F \quad \Rightarrow \quad F$$

(5) *reflexivity rule for* $\leq$:

$$u \leq u \quad \Rightarrow \quad \textit{true}.$$

Example: *max*1 *program*. Specification:

$$max1(a) \quad \Leftarrow \quad \textbf{achieve } a \leq z$$
$$\textbf{where } a \text{ is a number.}$$

The synthesis:

$$
\begin{array}{rll}
& \textbf{achieve } a \leqq z & \\
\Rightarrow & \textbf{achieve } a \leqq a & \\
& z \leftarrow a & \text{by assignment formation} \\
\Rightarrow & \textbf{prove } a \leqq a & \\
& z \leftarrow a & \text{by achieve-elimination} \\
\Rightarrow & \textbf{prove } \textit{true} & \\
& z \leftarrow a & \text{by reflexivity} \\
\Rightarrow & \Lambda & \\
& z \leftarrow a & \text{by prove elimination} \\
\Rightarrow & z \leftarrow a & \text{by composition identity.}
\end{array}
$$

C. Simultaneous-goal principle. In general, we cannot achieve a simultaneous goal by decomposing it into a sequence of goals, i.e.

$$
\textbf{achieve } P \text{ and } Q \quad \Rightarrow \quad
\begin{cases}
\textbf{achieve } P \\
\textbf{achieve } Q
\end{cases}
$$

or

$$
\textbf{achieve } P \text{ and } Q \quad \Rightarrow \quad
\begin{cases}
\textbf{achieve } Q \\
\textbf{achieve } P ,
\end{cases}
$$

because in the course of making the second condition true we may very well make the first false. We really need the *simultaneous-goal principle*

$$
\textbf{achieve } P \text{ and } Q \quad \Rightarrow \quad
\begin{cases}
\textbf{achieve } P \\
\textbf{achieve } Q \\
\textbf{prove } P.
\end{cases}
$$

Here, "**prove** P" assures us that P is protected while Q is achieved.

For this purpose, it is very convenient to use the weakest-precondition operator with the *regression rules*:

$$
\begin{cases}
F \\
\textbf{achieve } P
\end{cases}
\quad \Rightarrow \quad
\begin{cases}
\textbf{achieve } wp(F, P) \\
F
\end{cases}
$$

and

$$
\begin{cases}
F \\
\textbf{prove } P
\end{cases}
\quad \Rightarrow \quad
\begin{cases}
\textbf{prove } wp(F, P) \\
F
\end{cases}
$$

Thus, the goal

$$
\begin{array}{l}
F_1 \\
F_2 \\
\textbf{achieve } P \\
\textbf{prove } Q
\end{array}
$$

can be transformed to

$$\Rightarrow \quad \begin{array}{l} F_1 \\ \textbf{achieve } wp(F_2, P) \\ \textbf{prove } wp(F_2, Q) \\ F_2 \end{array}$$

and then to

$$\Rightarrow \quad \begin{array}{l} \textbf{achieve } wp(F_1, wp(F_2, P)) \\ \textbf{prove } wp(F_1, wp(F_2, Q)) \\ F_1 \\ F_2 . \end{array}$$

For example, suppose our goal is

$$\begin{array}{l} y \leftarrow x \\ y \leftarrow y + 1 \\ \textbf{achieve } y \geq 2 \\ \textbf{prove } x < y. \end{array}$$

An attempt to achieve the relation $y \geq 2$ by the assignment $y \leftarrow 2$ will fail, since we cannot prove $x < 2$:

$$\begin{array}{ll} y \leftarrow x & \\ y \leftarrow y + 1 & \\ \textbf{achieve } y \geq 2 \quad \Rightarrow \quad y \leftarrow 2 \\ \textbf{prove } x < y & \textit{failure.} \end{array}$$

However, it can be transformed to

$$\begin{array}{ll} y \leftarrow x & \\ \textbf{achieve } wp(y \leftarrow y+1, y \geq 2) = \textbf{achieve } y \geq 1 \quad \Rightarrow \quad y \leftarrow 1 \\ \textbf{prove } wp(y \leftarrow y+1, x < y) = \textbf{prove } x < y+1 & \textit{failure} \\ y \leftarrow y+1, & \end{array}$$

and then again

$$\begin{array}{ll} \textbf{achieve } wp(y \leftarrow x, y \geq 1) = \textbf{achieve } x \geq 1 \quad \Rightarrow \quad x \leftarrow 1 \\ \textbf{prove } wp(y \leftarrow x, x < y+1) = \textbf{prove } x < x+1 & \textit{success} \\ y \leftarrow x & \\ y \leftarrow y+1, & \end{array}$$

Therefore, the following program segment achieves the goal

$$\begin{array}{l} x \leftarrow 1 \\ y \leftarrow x \\ y \leftarrow y+1. \end{array}$$

D. Conditional-formation principle.

Example: $max\,2$ *program*. The goal:

$$max\,2(a, b) \quad \Leftarrow \quad \textbf{achieve } a \leq z \textbf{ and } b \leq z$$
$$\textbf{where } a \textbf{ and } b \textbf{ are numbers}$$

The synthesis:

achieve $a \leq z$ **and** $b \leq z$

$\Downarrow$ *simultaneous-goal principle*

achieve $a \leq z$
achieve $b \leq z$
prove $a \leq z$

$\Downarrow$ $max\,1$ *program*

$z \leftarrow a$
assert $a \leq z$
achieve $b \leq z$
prove $a \leq z$

achieve elimination
$z \leftarrow a$
assert $a \leq z$
prove $b \leq z$
prove $a \leq z$

$\Downarrow$

$z \leftarrow a$
prove $b \leq z$

$max\,1$ *program*
$z \leftarrow a$
assert $a \leq z$
$z \leftarrow b$
prove $a \leq z$

$\Downarrow$ *regression*

$z \leftarrow a$
assert $a \leq z$
prove $a \leq b$
$z \leftarrow b$

$\Downarrow$ *transitivity*

$z \leftarrow a$
prove $z \leq b$
$z \leftarrow b$

The last step is justified by the fact that in order to prove the goal $a \leq b$, when it is already known that $a \leq z$, it suffices to prove $z \leq b$.

We are going to use the *conditional-formation principle*:

if we have

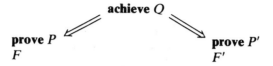

where P or P' is true and P is primitive, we may then transform it to

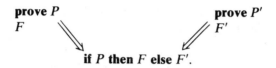

In the *max2* example therefore we have

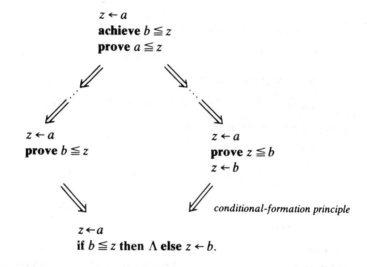

Thus

$$max2(a, b) \quad \Leftarrow \quad z \leftarrow a$$
$$\text{if } z < b \text{ then } z \leftarrow b.$$

E. Recursion-formation principle.

Example: simplified max program.

$$max(a, n) \quad \Leftarrow \quad \textbf{achieve } all(a[0:n]) \leq z$$
$$\qquad\qquad \text{and } z \in a[0:n]$$
$$\qquad\qquad \text{and only } z \text{ changed}$$
$$\qquad\qquad \textbf{where} \quad a \text{ is an array of numbers}$$
$$\qquad\qquad\qquad n \text{ is an integer}$$
$$\qquad\qquad\qquad 0 \leq n.$$

Since, in this example, we only attempt to illustrate how recursive calls are introduced, and not how the simultaneous-goal principle is applied, we consider a simplified goal

$$max(a, n) \quad \Leftarrow \quad \textbf{achieve} \ all(a[0:n]) \leq z$$
$$\textbf{where} \quad a \ \text{is an array of numbers}$$
$$n \ \text{is an integer}$$
$$0 \leq n.$$

Here we have the new *all* construct, where $P(all(a[u:w]))$ means $\forall i, u \leq i \leq w, P(a[i])$. Some of the *all* rules are

(1) the vacuous rule

$$P(all(a[u:w])) \quad \Rightarrow \quad true \quad \text{if } u > w;$$

(2) the singleton rule

$$P(all(a[u:w])) \quad \Rightarrow \quad P(a[u]) \quad \text{if } u = w;$$

(3) the right-decomposition rule

$$P(all(a[u:w])) \quad \Rightarrow \quad P(all(a[u:w-1])) \text{ and } P(a[w]) \quad \text{if } u < w;$$

(4) the left-decomposition rule

$$P(all(a[u:w])) \quad \Rightarrow \quad P(a[u]) \text{ and } P(all(a[u+1:w])) \quad \text{if } u < w.$$

The derivation starts as follows:

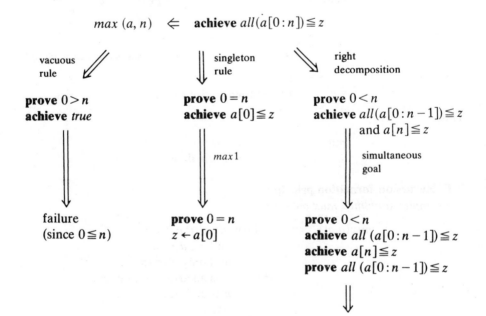

$$max \ (a, n) \quad \Leftarrow \quad \textbf{achieve} \ all(a[0:n]) \leq z$$

vacuous rule	singleton rule	right decomposition
prove $0 > n$ **achieve** *true*	**prove** $0 = n$ **achieve** $a[0] \leq z$	**prove** $0 < n$ **achieve** $all(a[0:n-1]) \leq z$ and $a[n] \leq z$
	$max\,1$	simultaneous goal
failure (since $0 \leq n$)	**prove** $0 = n$ $z \leftarrow a[0]$	**prove** $0 < n$ **achieve** $all\ (a[0:n-1]) \leq z$ **achieve** $a[n] \leq z$ **prove** $all\ (a[0:n-1]) \leq z$

The *recursion-formation principle* is of the form:

> If

$$f(x) \;\Leftarrow\; \textbf{achieve } P(x)$$
$$\textbf{where } Q(x)$$

goal: **achieve** $P(x)$

$$\vdots$$

subgoal: **achieve** $P(t)$

then

$$\textbf{achieve } P(t)$$
$$\Downarrow$$
$$f(t),$$

provided t is primitive, $Q(t)$ is satisfied (input condition) and $x > t$ in some well-founded ordering $>$ (termination condition).

Proceeding with our examples, we obtain

prove $0 < n$
achieve *all* $(a[0:n-1]) \le z$
achieve $a[n] \le z$
prove $all(a[0:n-1]) \le z$

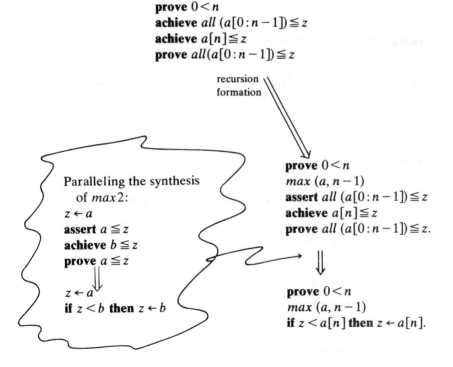

recursion
formation

prove $0 < n$
$max\,(a, n-1)$
assert *all* $(a[0:n-1]) \le z$
achieve $a[n] \le z$
prove *all* $(a[0:n-1]) \le z.$

$$\Downarrow$$

prove $0 < n$
$max\,(a, n-1)$
if $z < a[n]$ **then** $z \leftarrow a[n].$

Paralleling the synthesis
of $max\,2$:
$z \leftarrow a$
assert $a \le z$
achieve $b \le z$
prove $a \le z$

$$\Downarrow$$

$z \leftarrow a$
if $z < b$ **then** $z \leftarrow b$

Thus applying the conditional-formation rule, we obtain

$$max\,(a, n) \quad \Leftarrow \quad \textbf{achieve } all\,(a[0:n]) \leqq z$$

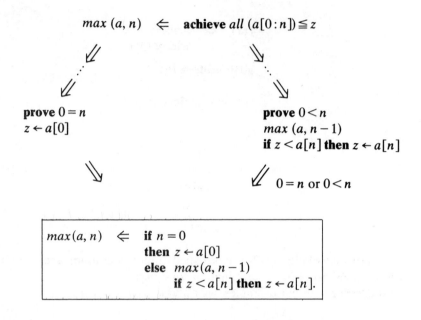

prove $0 = n$
$z \leftarrow a[0]$

prove $0 < n$
$max\,(a, n-1)$
if $z < a[n]$ **then** $z \leftarrow a[n]$

$0 = n$ or $0 < n$

$$
\begin{aligned}
max(a, n) \quad \Leftarrow \quad &\textbf{if } n = 0 \\
&\textbf{then } z \leftarrow a[0] \\
&\textbf{else } max(a, n-1) \\
&\quad \textbf{if } z < a[n] \textbf{ then } z \leftarrow a[n].
\end{aligned}
$$

F. Generalization. In the above example we have used the right-decomposition rule of *all*:

$$P(all(a[u:w])) \quad \Rightarrow \quad P(all(a[u:w-1])) \text{ and } P(a[w]) \quad \text{if } u < w.$$

Now, suppose we attempt to use the left-decomposition rule instead:

$$P(all(a[u:w])) \quad \Rightarrow \quad P(a[u]) \text{ and } P(all(a[u+1:w])) \quad \text{if } u < w.$$

Then we obtain

$$max\,(a, n) \quad \Leftarrow \quad \textbf{achieve } all\,(a[0:n]) \leqq z$$

prove $0 < n$
achieve $all\,(a[1:n]) \leqq z$
achieve $a[0] \leqq z$
prove $all\,(a[1:n]) \leqq z.$

We cannot apply the recursion-formation principle, since the top-level goal is $all(a[0:n]) \leq z$, while the subgoal is $all(a[1:n]) \leq z$. However, by generalization (0 becomes i and 1 becomes $i+1$) we obtain

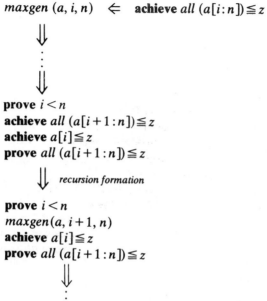

$$maxgen\,(a, i, n) \;\Leftarrow\; \textbf{achieve } all\,(a[i:n]) \leq z$$

$\Downarrow$

$\vdots$

$\Downarrow$

prove $i < n$
achieve $all\,(a[i+1:n]) \leq z$
achieve $a[i] \leq z$
prove $all\,(a[i+1:n]) \leq z$

$\Downarrow$ *recursion formation*

prove $i < n$
$maxgen(a, i+1, n)$
achieve $a[i] \leq z$
prove $all\,(a[i+1:n]) \leq z$

$\Downarrow$

$\vdots$

The final program is

$$
\begin{aligned}
&max(a, n) \;\Leftarrow\; maxgen(a, 0, n)\\
&\textbf{where}\\
&maxgen(a, i, n) \;\Leftarrow\; \textbf{if } i = n\\
&\qquad\qquad\qquad\qquad \textbf{then } z \leftarrow a[i]\\
&\qquad\qquad\qquad\qquad \textbf{else } maxgen(a, i+1, n)\\
&\qquad\qquad\qquad\qquad\quad \textbf{if } z < a[i] \textbf{ then } z \leftarrow a[i].
\end{aligned}
$$

G. Program modification. Suppose we also want to find the index of the maximal element in the example *max* above. Then, by modifying the $max(a, n)$ program we obtain

$$max\,(a, n) \;\Leftarrow\; \textbf{achieve } all\,(a[0:n]) \leq z \text{ and } z = a[y]$$

$\Downarrow$ *simultaneous goal*

achieve $all\,(a[0:n]) \leq z$
achieve $z = a[y]$
prove $all(a[0:n]) \leq z$

$\Downarrow$

$$max\ (a, n)$$
assert $all\ (a[0:n]) \leqq z$
achieve $z = a[y]$
prove $all\ (a[0:n]) \leqq z$

$$\Downarrow$$
$$\vdots$$
$$\Downarrow$$

$max\ (a, n) \quad \Leftarrow \quad$ **if** $n = 0$
            then $z \leftarrow a[0]$
                    assert $z = a[0]$
                    achieve $z = a[y]$
                    prove $a[0] \leqq z$
            else $max(a, n - 1)$
                    assert $all(a[0:n-1]) \leqq z$
                    if $z < a[n]$ **then** $z \leftarrow a[n]$
                                    assert $z = a[n]$
                                    achieve $z = a[y]$
                                    prove $all\ (a[0:n]) \leqq z$

$$\vdots$$
$$\Downarrow$$

$max(a, n) \quad \Leftarrow \quad$ **if** $n = 0$
            then $z \leftarrow a[0]$
                    $y \leftarrow 0$ ◄
            else $max(a, n - 1)$
                    if $z < a[n]$ **then** $z \leftarrow a[n]$
                                    $y \leftarrow n$ ◄

H. Comparison with structured programming. Let us consider the synthesis of an $exp(x, y)$ program which sets the value of a variable z to be the exponential $z = x^y$ of two integers x and y, where $x > 0$ and $y \geqq 0$. We are given a number of properties of the exponential function:

$$u^v = 1 \qquad\qquad \text{if } u \neq 0 \text{ and } v = 0,$$
$$u^v = (u \cdot u)^{v \div 2} \qquad \text{if } v \text{ is even, and}$$
$$u^v = u \cdot (u \cdot u)^{v \div 2} \qquad \text{if } v \text{ is odd,}$$

for any integers u and v. Here, $\div$ denotes integer division.

1. *Constructing an iterative program* (*by the structured-programming approach*). Written in our notation, the top-level goal of a structured programming derivation is

$$\text{Goal A: } \textbf{achieve } z = x^y,$$

assuming that x^y is a nonprimitive construct which may not appear in the final program. This goal can be decomposed into the conjunction of two conditions

$$\text{Goal B: } \textbf{achieve } z \cdot xx^{yy} = x^y \text{ and } yy = 0.$$

The motivation for this step is that, initially, we can achieve the first condition $z \cdot xx^{yy} = x^y$ easily enough (by setting xx to x, yy to y, and z to 1); thus, if we manage to achieve the second condition $yy = 0$ subsequently, while maintaining the first condition, we will have achieved our goal.

For this purpose, we establish an iterative loop, whose invariant in $z \cdot xx^{yy} = x^y$ and whose exit condition is $yy = 0$; the body of the loop must bring yy closer to zero while maintaining the invariant.

$$(xx, yy, z) \leftarrow (x, y, 1)$$
while $yy \neq 0$
do assert $z \cdot xx^{yy} = x^y$
    achieve reduction in yy
        while maintaining invariant.

By exploiting the known properties of the exponential and other arithmetic functions, we are led ultimately to the final program

$$exp(x, y) \iff (xx, yy, z) \leftarrow (x, y, 1)$$
    while $yy \neq 0$
    do assert $z \cdot xx^{yy} = x^y$
      if $even(yy)$
      then $(xx, yy) \leftarrow (xx \cdot xx, yy \div 2)$.
      else $(xx, yy, z) \leftarrow (xx \cdot xx, yy \div 2, xx \cdot z)$.

The weak point in this derivation seems to be the passage from Goal A to Goal B. This step is necessary to provide the invariant for the loop of the ultimate program, but requires considerable insight.

2. *Constructing a recursive program* (*by the above synthesis approach*). The derivation of the corresponding recursive program by the program-synthesis technique is straightforward. By using the same properties of the arithmetic

functions that were exploited in the structured-programming derivation, we can derive

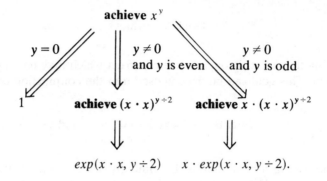

$$exp(x \cdot x, y \div 2) \qquad x \cdot exp(x \cdot x, y \div 2).$$

Thus, only after we observe that the subexpression $(x \cdot x)^{y \div 2}$ is an instance of the expression x^y, do we actually decide to introduce a recursive call $exp(x \cdot x, y \div 2)$ to compute this subexpression. Since $0 \leqq y \div 2 < y$, the resulting $exp(x, y)$ program must terminate.

$$exp(x, y) \quad \Leftarrow \quad \textbf{if } y = 0$$
$$\textbf{then } 1$$
$$\textbf{else if } even \ (y)$$
$$\textbf{then } exp(x \cdot x, y \div 2)$$
$$\textbf{else } x \cdot exp(x \cdot x, y \div 2).$$

CHAPTER 6

Termination of Production Systems

(Manna and Ness (1970), Dershowitz and Manna (1979))

The following is a production system that differentiates with respect to x an expression containing $+$ and $\cdot$,

1. $Dx \;\; \rightsquigarrow \;\; 1$
2. $Dy \;\; \rightsquigarrow \;\; 0$
3. $D(\alpha + \beta) \;\; \rightsquigarrow \;\; D\alpha + D\beta$
4. $D(\alpha \cdot \beta) \;\; \rightsquigarrow \;\; (\beta \cdot D\alpha) + (\alpha \cdot D\beta),$

where y can be any constant or variable other than x.

Let us consider the expression

$$D(D(x \cdot x) + y).$$

We could either apply the third production to the outer D, or else we could apply the fourth production to the inner D, and so on, obtaining Fig. 1. The left path, for example, is denoted by

$$D(D(x \cdot x) + y) \rightarrow D((x \cdot Dx + x \cdot Dx) + y) \rightarrow D(x \cdot Dx + x \cdot Dx) + Dy \rightarrow \cdots .$$

In general, at each stage of the computation there are many ways to proceed, and the choice is made nondeterministically. In our case, all choices eventually lead to the expression

$$((1 \cdot 1 + x \cdot 0) + (1 \cdot 1 + x \cdot 0)) + 0,$$

for which no further application of a production is possible.

DEFINITION. A production system π over a set of expressions E terminates if there exists no infinite sequence $e_1 \rightarrow e_2 \rightarrow e_3 \rightarrow \cdots$ of expressions in E such that every e_{i+1} results from e_i by the application of a rule. In other words, given any expression e_1 in E, all possible executions that start with e_1 reach a state for which there is no way to continue applying productions.

It is difficult to prove the termination of such a system because (1) a production (e.g. the last two in the differentiation example above) may increase the size of an expression; (2) a production (e.g. the fourth) may actually duplicate occurrences of subexpressions; (3) a production may affect not only the structure of the subexpression it is applied to, but it may also change the set of productions which match its superexpressions. We must take into consideration the many different possible sequences, generated by the nondeterministic choice of productions and subexpressions.

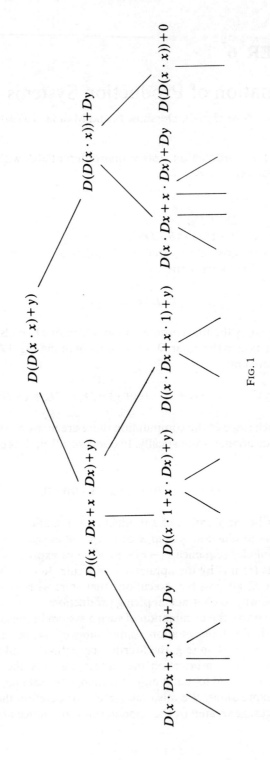

FIG. 1

THEOREM. *A production system π over E terminates if and only if there exists a well-founded set $(W, >)$, and a termination function $\tau: E \to W$, such that for any $e, e' \in E$*

$$e \to e' \quad \Rightarrow \quad \tau(e) > \tau(e').$$

A. Example 1: Associativity. Consider the production system

$$(\alpha + \beta) + \gamma \quad \leadsto \quad \alpha + (\beta + \gamma).$$

Note that the size of the expression is unchanged.

Regular termination proof: Take

$$(N, >) \quad \text{and} \quad \tau(e): E \to N \text{ such that} \quad \tau(\alpha + \beta) = 2 \cdot \tau(\alpha) + \tau(\beta)$$

$$\tau(atom) = 1.$$

Thus,

$$\tau((a + 3) + ((b + 1) + c)) = 2(2 \cdot 1 + 1) + (2(2 \cdot 1 + 1) + 1) = 13.$$

1. τ decreases

$$\tau((\alpha + \beta) + \gamma) \qquad\qquad \tau(\alpha + (\beta + \gamma))$$
$$\| \qquad\qquad\qquad\qquad \|$$
$$4\tau(\alpha) + 2\tau(\beta) + \tau(\gamma) > 2\tau(\alpha) + 2\tau(\beta) + \tau(\gamma),$$

since $\tau(\alpha) \geq 1$.

2. τ is monotonic in each operand

$$\tau(e_1) > \tau(e_2) \quad \Rightarrow \quad \begin{cases} \tau(e_1 + e_3) > \tau(e_2 + e_3) \\ \tau(e_3 + e_1) > \tau(e_3 + e_2). \end{cases}$$

Thus, if $e \to e'$ for the outer expression e, then some subexpression $(\alpha + \beta) + \gamma$ of e has been replaced by $\alpha + (\beta + \gamma)$ to obtain e'. We have $\tau((\alpha + \beta) + \gamma) > \tau(\alpha + (\beta + \gamma))$, by the first property. Therefore, by the monotonicity property we get $\tau(e) > \tau(e')$ for the outer expression. That is

$$e \to e' \quad \Rightarrow \quad \tau(e) > \tau(e').$$

Multiset proof (see Chapter 2): Take

$$(\mathcal{M}(N), \gg) \quad \text{and} \quad \tau(e) \text{ to be } \{|\alpha|: \alpha + \beta \text{ in } e\},$$

i.e., $\tau(e)$ is the multiset of the sizes (=number of symbols) of all left components of $+$ in e. Thus

$$\tau((a + 3) + ((b + 1) + c)) = \{1, 3, 1, 3\}.$$

$$\vdots \quad \vdots \quad \vdots \quad \vdots$$
$$1 \quad 3 \quad 1 \quad 3$$

1. τ decreases

$$\tau((\alpha+\beta)+\gamma) \qquad\qquad \tau(\alpha+(\beta+\gamma))$$
$$\|\qquad\qquad\qquad\qquad\qquad\|$$
$$\{|\alpha|,\ |\alpha+\beta|,\cdots\}\ \gg\ \{|\alpha|,|\beta|,\cdots\}.$$

That is, $\tau((\alpha+\beta)+\gamma)$ is the multiset consisting of $|\alpha|$, $|\alpha+\beta|$, and the sizes of left components of all inner $+$'s in α, β and γ; while $\tau(\alpha+(\beta+\gamma))$ is the same but with $|\alpha+\beta|$ replaced by the smaller element $|\beta|$.

2. Size is maintained

$$|(\alpha+\beta)+\gamma|=|\alpha+(\beta+\gamma)|;$$

therefore the sizes of the left components of higher-level $+$'s are not changed. Thus,

$$e\to e'\ \Rightarrow\ \tau(e)\gg\tau(e').\quad\square$$

B. Example 2: Distribution system. Consider

$$\alpha\cdot(\beta+\gamma)\ \rightsquigarrow\ (\alpha\cdot\beta)+(\alpha\cdot\gamma)$$
$$(\beta+\gamma)\cdot\alpha\ \rightsquigarrow\ (\beta\cdot\alpha)+(\gamma\cdot\alpha).$$

Note that the size of the expression is increased in both cases.

Regular proof: Take

$$(N,>)\quad\text{and}\quad \tau(e)\colon E\to N\quad\text{where}\ \tau(\alpha+\beta)=\tau(\alpha)+\tau(\beta)+1$$
$$\tau(\alpha\cdot\beta)=\tau(\alpha)\cdot\tau(\beta)$$
$$\tau(atom)=2.$$

Then

$$\tau((a+3)\cdot((b+1)\cdot c))=(2+2+1)\cdot((2+2+1)\cdot2)=50.$$

1. τ decreases

$$\tau(\alpha\cdot(\beta+\gamma)) \qquad\qquad \tau((\alpha\cdot\beta)+(\alpha\cdot\gamma))$$
$$\|\qquad\qquad\qquad\qquad\qquad\qquad\|$$
$$\tau(\alpha)\cdot\tau(\beta)+\tau(\alpha)\cdot\tau(\gamma)+\tau(\alpha)\ >\ \tau(\alpha)\cdot\tau(\beta)+\tau(\alpha)\cdot\tau(\gamma)+1,$$

since $\tau(\alpha)>1$; and similarly for the other production.

2. τ is monotonic in each operand

$$\tau(e_1)>\tau(e_2)\ \Rightarrow\ \begin{cases}\tau(e_1+e_3)>\tau(e_2+e_3)\\ \tau(e_3+e_1)>\tau(e_3+e_2)\\ \tau(e_1\cdot e_3)>\tau(e_2\cdot e_3)\\ \tau(e_3\cdot e_1)>\tau(e_3\cdot e_2).\end{cases}$$

Therefore

$$e \to e' \quad \Rightarrow \quad \tau(e) > \tau(e').$$

Multiset proof: Take

$$(\mathcal{M}(N), \gg) \quad \text{and} \quad \tau(e) \text{ to be } \{val(\alpha \cdot \beta): \alpha \cdot \beta \text{ in } e\},$$

where $val(e)$ is the arithmetic value of e with 1 for all atoms. Thus

$$\tau((a \cdot 3) \cdot ((b+1) \cdot c)) = \{val(a \cdot 3), val((a \cdot 3) \cdot ((b+1) \cdot c)), val((b+1) \cdot c)\}$$
$$= \{1 \cdot 1, 1 \cdot 2, 2 \cdot 1\}$$
$$= \{1, 2, 2\}.$$

1. τ decreases

$$
\begin{array}{ccc}
\tau(\alpha \cdot (\beta + \gamma)) & & \tau((\alpha \cdot \beta) + (\alpha \cdot \gamma)) \\
\| & & \| \\
\{val(\alpha \cdot (\beta + \gamma)), \cdots\} & \gg & \{val(\alpha \cdot \beta), val(\alpha \cdot \gamma), \cdots\} \\
\nearrow \uparrow \nwarrow & & \nearrow \uparrow \nwarrow \\
\tau(\alpha) \; \tau(\beta) \; \tau(\gamma) & & \tau(\alpha) \; \tau(\beta) \; \tau(\gamma)
\end{array}
$$

2. value is maintained

$$val(\alpha \cdot (\beta + \gamma)) = val((\alpha \cdot \beta) + (\alpha \cdot \gamma));$$

and similarly for the other production.
Therefore

$$e \to e' \quad \Rightarrow \quad \tau(e) \gg \tau(e'). \quad \square$$

C. Example 3: Differentiation system. Consider

$$
\begin{array}{lcl}
Dx & \leadsto & 1 \\
Dy & \leadsto & 0 \\
D(\alpha + \beta) & \leadsto & D\alpha + D\beta \\
D(\alpha \cdot \beta) & \leadsto & \alpha \cdot D\beta + \beta \cdot D\alpha \\
D(\ln \alpha) & \leadsto & (D\alpha)/\alpha \\
D(-\alpha) & \leadsto & -(D\alpha) \\
D(\alpha - \beta) & \leadsto & D\alpha - D\beta \\
D(\alpha/\beta) & \leadsto & (D\alpha/\beta) - ((\alpha \cdot D\beta)/(\beta{\uparrow}2)) \\
D(\alpha{\uparrow}\beta) & \leadsto & D\alpha \cdot \beta \cdot (\alpha{\uparrow}(\beta - 1)) + D\beta \cdot \ln \alpha \cdot (\alpha{\uparrow}\beta).
\end{array}
$$

Regular proof: Take

$$(N, >) \quad \text{and} \quad \tau(e): E \to N \text{ where } \quad \tau(\alpha \otimes \beta) = \tau(\alpha) + \tau(\beta)$$
$$\tau(D\alpha) = \tau(\alpha)^2$$
$$\tau(-\alpha) = \tau(\alpha) + 1$$
$$\tau(\ln \alpha) = \tau(\alpha) + 1$$
$$\tau(atom) = 4,$$

where $\otimes$ stands for any of the binary operations.

1. τ decreases

$$\pi_i \, \mathcal{N} \, \pi_i' \quad \Rightarrow \quad \tau(\pi_i) > \tau(\pi_i')$$

for every production. For example

$$\tau(D(\alpha/\beta))$$
$$\|$$
$$(\tau(\alpha) + \tau(\beta))^2$$
$$\|$$
$$\tau(\alpha)^2 + \tau(\beta)^2 + 2\tau(\alpha) \cdot \tau(\beta) \quad > \quad$$

$$\tau((D\alpha/\beta) - ((\alpha \cdot D\beta)/(\beta \uparrow 2)))$$
$$\|$$
$$(\tau(\alpha)^2 + \tau(\beta)) + (\tau(\alpha) + \tau(\beta)^2) + (\tau(\beta) + 4)$$
$$\|$$
$$\tau(\alpha)^2 + \tau(\beta)^2 + \tau(\alpha) + 2\tau(\beta) + 4,$$

since $\tau(\alpha), \tau(\beta) \geqq 4$.

2. τ is monotonic in each operand.
Therefore

$$e \to e' \quad \Rightarrow \quad \tau(e) > \tau(e').$$

Multiset proof: Since each production replaces an occurrence of D by one or more occurrences of D with shorter arguments, let us take

$$(\mathcal{M}(N), \gg) \quad \text{and} \quad \tau(e) \text{ to be } \{|\alpha|: D\alpha \text{ in } e\}.$$

1. τ decreases

$$\pi_i \, \mathcal{N} \, \pi_i' \quad \Rightarrow \quad \tau(\pi_i) \gg \tau(\pi_i')$$

for every production. For example

$$\tau(D(\alpha \cdot \beta)) \qquad \tau((\beta \cdot D\alpha) + (\alpha \cdot D\beta))$$
$$\| \qquad\qquad\qquad \|$$
$$\{|\alpha \cdot \beta|, \cdots\} \quad \gg \quad \{|\alpha|, |\beta|, \cdots\}$$
$$\nearrow \; \nwarrow \qquad\qquad \nearrow \nearrow \uparrow \nwarrow$$
$$\tau(\alpha) \; \tau(\beta) \qquad \tau(\beta) \; \tau(\alpha) \; \tau(\alpha) \; \tau(\beta)$$

2. However

$$|D(\alpha \cdot \beta)| < |(\beta \cdot D\alpha) + (\alpha \cdot D\beta)|;$$

therefore the proof does not work.

We need a stronger mathematical tool since we are losing vital information: the D's are nested in the expression, while our multiset is linear.

D. Nested multisets.

DEFINITION. A *nested multiset* over a set $\mathscr{S}$ is either an element of $\mathscr{S}$, or else it is a finite multiset of nested multisets over $\mathscr{S}$. We denote by $\mathscr{M}^*(\mathscr{S})$ the set of nested multisets over $\mathscr{S}$.

For example,

$$\{\{1, 1\}, \{\{0\}, 1, 2\}, 0\}$$

is a nested multiset over N.

Each element of a nested multiset is assigned a *depth* corresponding to the number of braces surrounding it. Thus

$$\{\{1, 1\}, \{\{0\}, 1, 2\}, 5\}$$

$$
\begin{array}{ccccc}
\vdots & \vdots & \vdots & \vdots & \vdots \\
\vdots & \vdots & \vdots & \vdots & \vdots \\
2 & 2 & 3 & 2\ 2 & 1 \cdots \text{depth.}
\end{array}
$$

This multiset is said to be of depth 3 since it contains at least one element of depth 3 and no element of greater depth.

For a given partially-ordered set $(\mathscr{S}, >)$, the *nested-multiset* ordering $\gg^*$ on $\mathscr{M}^*(\mathscr{S})$ is the recursive version of the standard multiset ordering: For two elements $M, M' \in \mathscr{M}^*(\mathscr{S})$ we say that

$$M \gg^* M'$$

if

1. $M, M' \in \mathscr{S}$ and $M > M'$ (two elements of the base set are compared using $>$), or else

2. $M \notin \mathscr{S}$ and $M' \in \mathscr{S}$ (any multiset is greater than any element of the base set), or else

3. $M, M' \notin \mathscr{S}$, and for some $X, Y, Z \in \mathscr{M}^*(\mathscr{S})$, where X is not empty,

$$M = X \cup Z \quad \text{and} \quad M' = Y \cup Z$$

and

$$(\forall y \in Y)(\exists x \in X)x \gg^* y.$$

For example, the nested multiset

$$\{\{1, 1\}, \{\{1\}, 1, 2\}, 0\}$$

is greater than

$$\{\{1, 0, 0\}, 5, \{1, 1, 2\}, 0\},$$

since $\{1, 1\}$ is greater than both $\{1, 0, 0\}$ and 5, and $\{\{1\}, 1, 2\}$ is greater than $\{1, 1, 2\}$. The nested multiset

$$\{\{1, 1\}, \{\{1\}, 1, 2\}, 0\}$$

is also greater than

$$\{\{\{0, 0\}, 7\}, \{5, 5, 2\}, 5\},$$

since $\{1, 1\}$ and 0 were removed, and $\{\{1\}, 1, 2\}$ is greater than each of the three elements $\{\{0, 0\}, 7\}$, $\{5, 5, 2\}$, and 5.

THEOREM. $(\mathcal{M}^*(\mathcal{S}), \gg^*)$ *is well-founded* $\Leftrightarrow$ $(\mathcal{S}, >)$ *is well founded.*

Let us consider again the differentiation system

$$
\begin{aligned}
Dx &\;\rightsquigarrow\; 1 \\
Dy &\;\rightsquigarrow\; 0 \\
D(\alpha + \beta) &\;\rightsquigarrow\; D\alpha + D\beta \\
D(\alpha \cdot \beta) &\;\rightsquigarrow\; D\beta + \beta \cdot D\alpha \\
D(\ln \alpha) &\;\rightsquigarrow\; (D\alpha)/\alpha \\
D(-\alpha) &\;\rightsquigarrow\; -(D\alpha) \\
D(\alpha - \beta) &\;\rightsquigarrow\; D\alpha - D\beta \\
D(\alpha/\beta) &\;\rightsquigarrow\; (D\alpha/\beta) - ((\alpha \cdot D\beta)/(\beta{\uparrow}2)) \\
D(\alpha{\uparrow}\beta) &\;\rightsquigarrow\; D\alpha \cdot \beta \cdot (\alpha{\uparrow}(\beta - 1)) + D\beta \cdot \ln \alpha \cdot (\alpha{\uparrow}\beta).
\end{aligned}
$$

For a nested multiset proof, we take

$$(\mathcal{M}^*(N), \gg^*) \quad \text{and} \quad \tau(e): E \to \mathcal{M}^*(N),$$

where for each occurrence of D in e we associate the size of its argument with the appropriate nesting. For example

$$\tau(\; D \; (D \; (Dx \cdot Dy) + Dy) / Dx)$$
$$\vdots \quad \vdots \quad \vdots \quad \quad \vdots \quad \quad \vdots$$
$$\{\{9, \{5, \{1\}, \; \{1\}\}, \; \{1\}\}, \; \{1\}\}.$$

1. Outer D's have lesser depth—they are dominated by the inner D's.
2. τ decreases

$$\pi_i \;\rightsquigarrow\; \pi_i' \quad \Rightarrow \quad \tau(\pi_i) \gg^* \tau(\pi_i')$$

for every production. For example

$$
\begin{array}{ccc}
\tau(D(\alpha \cdot \beta)) & & \tau((\beta \cdot D\alpha) + (\alpha \cdot D\beta)) \\
\| & & \| \\
\{\{|\alpha \cdot \beta|, \cdots\}\} & \gg^* & \{\cdots, \{|\alpha|, \cdots\}, \cdots, \{|\beta|, \cdots\}\}, \\
\nearrow \nwarrow & & \uparrow \quad\quad \uparrow \quad \uparrow \quad\quad\quad \uparrow \\
\tau(\alpha) \; \tau(\beta) & & \tau(\beta) \quad \tau(\alpha) \; \tau(\alpha) \quad\quad \tau(\beta)
\end{array}
$$

Since, $\{|\alpha \cdot \beta|, \cdots\}$ on the left-hand side is greater than any one of the components of the right-hand side.

Thus,

$$e \to e' \quad \Rightarrow \quad \tau(e) \gg^* \tau(e').$$

Acknowledgments. I would like to thank N. Dershowitz and R. Waldinger for their help in the preparation of these lecture notes. D. Dolev and P. Wolper provided valuable comments on the manuscript.

References

This list includes only the papers that were used directly in the preparation of these lecture notes. The reader can find an extensive bibliography in the survey by Manna and Waldinger (1978a).

R. M. BURSTALL (1974), *Program proving as hand simulation with a little induction*, Information Processing 1974, North-Holland, Amsterdam, pp. 308–312.

N. DERSHOWITZ AND Z. MANNA (1977), *Inference rules for program annotation*, technical report, Computer Science Dept., Stanford University, Stanford, CA.

—— (1979), *Proving termination with multiset orderings*, Comm. ACM, 22, pp. 465–476.

R. W. FLOYD (1967), *Assigning meanings to programs*, Proceedings of Symposium in Applied Mathematics, vol. 19, J. T. Schwartz, ed., American Mathematical Society, Providence, RI, pp. 19–32.

C. A. R. HOARE (1969), *An axiomatic basis of computer programming*, Comm. ACM, 12, pp. 576–580, 583.

Z. MANNA (1971), *Mathematical theory of partial correctness*, J. Comput. System Sci., 5, pp. 239–253.

Z. MANNA AND S. NESS (1970), *On the termination of Markov algorithms*, Proc. Third Hawaii International Conference on System Sciences (Honolulu, HI), pp. 789–792.

Z. MANNA AND R. WALDINGER (1979), *Synthesis: dreams ⇒ programs*, IEEE Trans. Software Engineering, SE-5, pp. 294–328.

—— (1978), *Is "sometime" sometimes better than "always"? Intermittent assertions in proving program correctness*, Comm. ACM, 21, pp. 159–172.

—— (1978a), *The logic of computer programming*, IEEE Trans. Software Engineering, SE-4, pp. 199–229.

J. H. MORRIS AND B. WEGBREIT (1977), *Subgoal induction*, Comm. ACM, 20, pp. 209–222.

8986128